DOGS

A Kid's Book of

DOG BREEDS

Written by Eve Heidi Bine-Stock
Illustrated by Jean Batzell Fitzgerald

Contents

What is a dog breed?

A dog breed is a type of dog that has a certain kind of personality and look. For example, a dog's personality may be playful or shy and their look may include a long bushy tail and floppy ears.

A mama-dog and papa-dog of the same breed have puppies with a similar personality and look as their parents.

Where do dog breeds come from?

There are over 400 different dog breeds worldwide and most of them originally descended from the wolf.

This is how it probably started: Long ago, human hunters probably found wolf cubs and took them home with them. As the cubs grew up around people, they became partially tamed. The more tame ones were kept and bred. Later, when people noticed a change in personality or look that occurred naturally in a relatively tame wolf, and they wanted to keep this new trait, they bred the wolves until the trait became stable and predictable. This is how new dog breeds originally came about.

In this book, we will learn about 20 of the most recognizable and popular dog breeds today.

German Shepherd

The German Shepherd is a big dog, noble and heroic.

German Shepherds help rescue teams find injured people who are trapped somewhere, such as a building that has fallen down.

In war-time, they find enemy soldiers and hidden weapons, and save our own wounded soldiers by pulling them to safety. German Shepherds even jump from aircraft, strapped to soldiers wearing parachutes. Then the dogs run ahead to hunt for the enemy. Tiny cameras are fixed to their heads to send images back to their human partners.

German Shepherds are also police dogs, called "K-9 cops," who chase and catch criminals who are running away or hiding.

And German Shepherds are famous for helping blind people. When they do this, they are called "seeing-eye dogs."

When German Shepherds are working, they are tough and brave, and will risk their lives for their human partners. When their workday is over, they relax and become friendly family dogs.

One German Shepherd named "Bronco" was an award-winning crime-fighter who even protected President George W. Bush when he came to town to visit, yet every year Bronco played with small children at the "Kops-n-Kids" Christmas party! This shows the many sides of the German Shepherd's personality.

The most famous German Shepherd was "Rin Tin Tin." He could jump almost 12 feet—that's probably higher than your living room ceiling.

He was a Hollywood movie star who received 10,000 fan letters a week! Rin Tin Tin is honored with his own star in the pavement of the Hollywood Walk of Fame.

Herbert Hoover's German Shepherd, "King Tut," helped him win the Presidential election because Americans fell in love with a campaign picture of King Tut "begging for votes" next to a smiling Hoover. President Franklin Delano Roosevelt—"FDR" for short—brought his German Shepherd, "Major," with him to live in the White House. And President John F. Kennedy had a German Shepherd named "Clipper." Kennedy made it America's goal to land on the moon by 1969—which we did!

An American President's dog is known as the country's "First Dog."

Origin

The German Shepherd breed originated from a chance meeting at a German dog show in 1899. A man saw a dog there, fell in love, bought him on the spot, and proclaimed him "the first German Shepherd Dog." All dogs of this breed descend from that special dog.

Who was that man? And what was that dog?

The man was a former veterinary student and ex-cavalry Captain, Max von Stephanitz. The dog he met was everything the Captain thought a working dog should be—strong, intelligent and loyal. The dog was perfect, except, apparently, for his name—the Captain changed it from "Hektor" to "Horand."

The Captain formed the Society for the German Shepherd Dog and bred Horand with other dogs to his strict standards. The Captain is considered the creator of the breed.

And what name did the Captain give to Horand's most successful pup? "Hektor"!

Golden Retriever

The Golden Retriever is a big dog, with kind eyes and a kind heart.

Golden Retrievers are patient and gentle with children, and love to run alongside you when you ride your bike. They also love to play "fetch." They are one of the world's favorite family dogs.

Golden Retrievers are very smart and can learn almost 250 different commands.

As therapy dogs, Golden Retrievers visit hospitals and nursing homes to cheer and comfort sick and frail patients of all ages.

As service dogs, Golden Retrievers help disabled people in many ways—by opening and closing doors, fetching drinks from the refrigerator, even carrying laundry to the washing machine!

Golden Retrievers also help police find illegal drugs called "narcotics" in suitcases at airports, cars at border crossings, and packages at the post office.

Many, many Golden Retrievers save lives. "Brandy" was an old Golden Retriever who was sadly left behind when her owner died of old age. Brandy was locked out of the home where she used to live, so she soon befriended a little boy in the neighborhood who fed her cookies.

The little boy, only a year-and-a-half old, one day disappeared.

His parents, the neighbors, and the police all searched frantically for six hours, but couldn't find him. Imagine how worried his parents were!

Then a police officer remembered that he had heard the faint sound of barking in the woods nearby. Could Brandy be with the little boy? Indeed, she was. When the police found them, Brandy was pressing the little boy against a tree with her shoulder so he wouldn't fall into a stream 35 feet below. Brandy had held the little boy there with all her strength for six full hours! When help finally came, Brandy let go and fell on the ground, weak, tired and satisfied. She had saved the little boy's life.

To thank Brandy, the little boy and his parents adoped her, and they all lived together as a family happily ever after.

One famous Golden Retriever you may know is "Buddy," star of the movie *Air Bud* and its sequels. In each movie, Buddy plays a different sport, including basketball, football, soccer, baseball and beach volleyball.

American President Gerald Ford had a Golden Retriever named "Liberty" who stayed by his side while he worked in the Oval Office of the White House.

Origin

In 1865, a Scottish gentleman named "Sir Dudley Marjoribanks" visited a cobbler in England, who had one yellow puppy in a litter of black retriever pups. Sir Marjoribanks fell in love with the yellow pup, named "Nous," and brought him home to his estate in Scotland.

Sir Marjoribanks bred Nous to achieve his idea of the best hunting dog—vigorous and powerful, yet gentle and easy to train—and always yellow.

The Golden Retriever was bred to fetch land birds such as pheasant and quail, and water birds such as ducks and geese—that's why Golden Retrievers love water.

They were also bred to have a soft mouth so they could bring the game back to their owners undamaged.

Sir Marjoribanks was later known as "Lord Tweedmouth." Both are funny names for a superb breeder!

Poodle

The Poodle comes in three sizes: large, small and tiny, or Standard, Miniature and Toy. The bigger the Poodle, the calmer he is. The Standard Poodle is very good with children, and the Toy Poodle loves to play "fetch."

Poodles are posh and poised, with a thoughful expression.

They come in different solid colors, including white, apricot, brown, grey and black. They have a curly coat that doesn't shed much, so Poodles are good for people with allergies. Some people call their coat "hair," rather than "fur."

Poodles are very smart and can learn many tricks. You may have seen a Toy Poodle performing at a circus.

The large Standard Poodle was originally a water retriever dog that fetched water birds, like ducks, for hunters. That special Poodle clip you often see was likely invented by hunters to help the Poodle swim better. They shaved the rear half of the dog so his thick coat wouldn't weigh him down, and left bracelets and pom-poms of hair elsewhere to protect his organs and joints from the cold.

Did you know that all-sized Poodles today have webbed feet? This is a reminder of their origin as water dogs.

Today, most Poodles are companion dogs, and often participate in dog shows for their beauty and obedience skills.

Two famous Poodles you may know are "Cleo" in *Clifford the Big Red Dog*, and "Foo-Foo," Miss Piggy's dog in *The Muppet Show*.

Winston Churchill, Prime Minister of England during World War II, owned a Poodle named "Rufus."

Origin

The Poodle breed is hundreds of years old. The large Standard Poodle came first, and the smaller sizes were bred soon after.

Some people say the Poodle originated in France, where they call him the "Caniche," (pronounced kan-eesh'), or "duck dog."

Other people say the Poodle originated in Germany because the German word "Pudel" means to splash in water. It's easy to see how "Pudel" is related to our English word, "puddle."

While the large Standard Poodle was bred as a water retriever, the Miniature Poodle used his keen sense of smell to find truffles in the woods. A truffle is a rare type of mushroom that is a special treat for people to eat.

For centuries, European kings and queens loved to keep Toy Poodles as pampered pets.

The Poodle is the national dog of France.

Beagle

The Beagle is a small hound, with big, soulful eyes that have a pleading look. The Beagle is friendly, good-natured and gentle. He plays well with children and other dogs, and is a popular family dog.

Beagles have a keen sense of smell and can follow a trail on the ground. They were originally bred to hunt wild rabbits.

Today, security agents at airports use the Beagle's sniffing skills to find forbidden food hidden in luggage. This is an important job for the Beagle because some travelers returning from exotic lands bring back food that carries diseases which can infect local crops and animals. The determined Beagle keeps this from happening.

Beagles also work after a fire has been put out, sniffing for chemicals that might have been used to make the fire spread faster. If these chemicals are found, police know that the fire was set on purpose, which is a serious crime called "arson."

One Beagle named "Belle" won an award for saving her owner's life, thanks to her sniffing ability. The owner had an illness called "diabetes," which means he had a problem regulating the sugar level in his body. The Beagle could tell by her nose when there was a change in her owner's sugar level. One day, the owner passed out due to a bad sugar level, so the Beagle dialed 911 on a cell phone with her teeth and barked at the emergency operator who answered! Help came right away and her owner was saved.

With their mild and merry manner, Beagles also act as therapy dogs to cheer up patients at hospitals and nursing homes.

Did you know that a ship was named after the Beagle? Charles Darwin, an Englishman who was famous for studying nature in the 1800s, took a five-year voyage on a ship called the "HMS Beagle." That's how popular Beagles were back then, too.

The most famous Beagle is the cartoon character, "Snoopy."

American President Lyndon Johnson had many Beagles—including one named "Him" and one named "Her"—and used to take them on walks around the White House lawn while he talked to reporters.

Origin

Beagle-like dogs go all the way back to Ancient Greece—that's about 2,500 years ago!

Henry VIII, King of England in the 1500s, and his daughter, Queen Elizabeth I, had packs of tiny Beagles called "Glove Beagles" and "Pocket Beagles." Elizabeth entertained her royal court with her "singing Beagles" by letting them play on the dinner table! The Beagle has a loud, baying cry that hunters love to hear, but can bother your family and neighbors.

The Beagle was even written about by William Shakespeare, the world's most famous English poet and playwright who lived in the late 1500s and early 1600s.

The modern breed of Beagle that we know today was standardized in America in the late 1800s and early 1900s—about the same time that the electric light bulb was invented and the first airplane flew.

The Beagle is now one of America's most popular breed of dog.

Collie

This big, beautiful dog is one of the world's favorites. The Collie is kind, gentle, loving and loyal.

One Collie named "Bobbie" traveled 2,000 miles in winter to find his family again after being separated from them during a vacation. Imagine the hardship Bobbie went through! This shows how devoted the Collie is to the ones he loves.

Another Collie named "Tang" saved four children by rushing into a street full of oncoming traffic and pushing the children to safety! For this act of heroism, Tang won the first Ken-L-Ration Gold Medal for America's Dog Hero of the Year. Since then, many other Collies have won the Gold Medal for their bravery.

The Collie's sense of hearing is very keen. People say that Collies "know when a storm is coming," because they can hear one while it is still far away.

Collies make great companions, especially for children. They also work as guide dogs for the blind, and appear in dog shows for their skill in obedience and herding.

The most famous Collie is "Lassie," star of movies and television. Lassie is even honored with a star on the pavement of the Hollywood Walk of Fame.

American President Calvin Coolidge had two snow-white Collies named "Rob Roy" and "Prudence Prim."

Origin

The Collie originated centuries ago in the northern hills of Scotland where he herded black-faced sheep. The word "black" in the old Scottish Gaelic language was "colley," so people called the dogs Collies, after the type of sheep they herded.

Sometimes the Collie is called the Scottish Collie.

The long, thick coat of the "rough" Collie like Lassie protected him from the cold and windy weather in the northern highlands of Scotland. There is also a "smooth" Collie with a short coat, suited for the warmer weather and wet marshes of the southern lowlands of Scotland. The Lassie-like Collie is much more popular in America.

Once, in 1860, when Queen Victoria of England visited Balmoral Castle in Scotland, she saw the Lassie-like Collie and fell in love. She brought the dog back with her to England, where the breed became very popular.

The 1943 movie *Lassie Come Home* made the Collie famous and beloved worldwide. Ever since, people couldn't get enough of Lassie, so the Collie has appeared almost non-stop in movies and television.

Chihuahua

The Chihuahua (say "chi-WAH-wah") is a tiny dog, usually weighing no more than a bag of flour. He is the smallest dog breed in the world. Some Chihuahuas are so small, they can stand on a person's open hand! Sometimes you may see a lady carrying a Chihuahua in her open purse.

The Chihuahua has big ears that stand straight up. He can have a short or long coat. The Chihuahua is bold and lively. People say he has a "saucy" expression.

You have to be careful to show this tiny dog that you are the boss—the "pack leader"—or else he will behave badly, snapping and yapping at people and other, much bigger dogs.

Believe it or not, three tiny chihuahuas cornered a full-grown mountain lion that had wandered into the garage of their family's home in California. They kept yapping until the game warden came and took the angry, hissing mountain lion away.

While Chihuahuas make good pets in a small apartment, they should not be kept indoors all the time. They need to go out for a walk or romp every day. The exercise helps them stay calm.

The Chihuahua hates cold weather and likes to wear a sweater to keep warm.

Unfortunately, the Chihuahua does not make a good pet for children unless they are very gentle and patient.

One famous Chihuahua is "Tinkerbell," Paris Hilton's pet. Another, "Coco," belongs to the famous dog trainer, Cesar Millan, who has a TV show called "The Dog Whisperer."

Origin

This breed gets his name from the Mexican state of Chihuahua, which borders on Texas, Arizona and New Mexico in the south-western United States.

Long before Columbus discovered America, the ancestors of the Chihuahua lived in Mexico and were considered sacred to the native Indians.

The Chihuahua's ancestors used to be bigger, but were bred with miniature Chinese dogs brought to Mexico by the Spanish Conquistadors—Spanish soldiers who defeated the Indian civilization in Mexico. The result was a much smaller Chihuahua, closer to the dog we know today.

Dalmatian

The Dalmatian is lean and elegant—quite a dashing figure, indeed! His trademark is his white coat with random spots of all black or all brown. The spots are between the size of a dime and a half-dollar. The spots are smaller on the smaller parts of his body, like his head, legs and tail, and bigger on bigger areas like his chest, back, sides and stomach. He even has spots inside his mouth and on the bottom of his paws!

A Dalmatian puppy is born pure white and it takes about two weeks for the spots on his coat to appear. He grows up to be a medium-sized dog.

Dalmatians can run, run, run for miles without getting tired. They are very playful and enjoy romping with children, but may be too rowdy for a toddler. Dalmatians love the company of people, so don't leave them alone too long or they'll become sad.

The Dalmatian likes to swim. He also likes to keep clean, so while he enjoys water, he may avoid stepping in a dirty puddle.

Today, the Dalmatian is famous for being the mascot of fire-fighters. The dog lives in the firehouse and gets to ride on the fire truck!

If you ever saw the popular Disney movie, *101 Dalmatians*, you probably still see spots before your eyes!

Origin

Way, way back in Ancient Egypt—about 5,700 years ago—King Cheops had a spotted pet dog. That's the earliest known dog like today's Dalmatian. King Cheops was famous for building the Great Pyramid of Giza.

Pictures of ancient Roman chariots show spotted dogs running alongside.

Much later, in the 1500s and 1600s—the period in Europe called the Renaissance—Dalmatians were popular performers in traveling circuses.

Later still, in the 1800s, Dalmatians were famous in England as "carriage dogs." They trotted alongside or underneath horse-drawn carriages. They could trot for 30 miles without tiring. When the driver stopped his carriage for a short break, or even overnight, he left it and the horses in the care of the Dalmatian, who would protect his charge against thieves. Horses and Dalmatians are natural friends. Just having a Dalmatian nearby keeps horses calm.

In the days before automobiles, when fire trucks were drawn by horses, Dalmatians went along with the fire trucks, just as they did with the carriages. Firefighters loved the Dalmatians so much that when their fire trucks became motorized, they still kept their Dalmatians. That's why Dalmatians are today known as the "firehouse dog."

Cocker Spaniel

American families love this small dog. And no wonder—he's merry, eager to please, and likes children and other pets.

When he gets excited, he wags his tail, and his whole tushie, too!

Be careful to keep his long ears from falling into the water or food bowl where they'll get wet or dirty. Just use deep, narrow bowls so his ears fall to the side of the bowls instead.

The Cocker Spaniel's gentle nature makes him a great therapy dog. Sick and frail patients feel better after a visit from this happy, loving dog.

In England, doctors use Cocker Spaniels to find cancer cells. Cancer is an illness where harmful cells grow in the body and push away and destroy healthy cells. Cocker Spaniels—especially one named "Tangle"—are very good at sniffing out the harmful cells and have saved people's lives.

Kids hardly ever get this illness.

One famous Cocker Spaniel you may know is "Lady" in the Disney movie *Lady and the Tramp*.

Another Cocker Spaniel named "Chota Peg" lived for 13 years on an American ocean liner and sailed two million ocean miles!

The name "Chota Peg" means "small drink" in slang used by sailors.

American President Rutherford B. Hayes had a Cocker Spaniel named "Dot."

Origin

The Cocker Spaniel gets his name from the "woodcock," a type of bird that people used to hunt for sport. The dog flushed the woodcock out of the brush and up into the air for his master to see. As far back as the 1300s, people referred to the "Spanyell" sporting dog.

Legend says that a Cocker Spaniel sailed on the Mayflower with the Pilgrims and arrived at Plymouth Rock in 1620. He was the first Cocker Spaniel to set paw in the New World, making his home here more than 150 years before America declared independence from England.

The American Cocker Spaniel developed differently from the English Cocker Spaniel and the two breeds were declared independent in 1935. The English Cocker Spaniel, seen in the picture below, is a bit bigger than the American and has a more hound-like head, with a longer muzzle.

What else happened in 1935? The game board "Monopoly" was first played, baseball star Babe Ruth hit his 714th and last home run of his career, and Amelia Earhart was first to fly a plane alone across the Pacific Ocean from California to Hawaii.

Yorkshire Terrier

This tiny dog's nickname is "Yorkie." Yorkies are spunky and bold, with sparkling eyes. They love to run and play, and are always busy and curious. They wag their tails all the time!

Yorkies are full of energy, which is good for kids, but they become snappy if young kids tease them too much, so Yorkies are better for older, more considerate children.

Yorkies make great watchdogs. They are very brave. One Yorkie named "Oliver" heard a rumpus outside and pushed open the screen door of his home to check out what was happening. Then he saw it: a big dog was attacking an old lady! Without a second thought, Oliver raced to the rescue. He snapped and growled at the big dog, who stopped hurting the old lady and went after tiny Oliver. Oliver dashed to safety under a parked car, and later needed only nine stitches.

Another tiny Yorkie named "Smoky" was actually a war hero! She was found on a battlefield during World War II, on an island in the Pacific Ocean where the Americans were fighting the Japanese. An American soldier adopted her and by his side, Smoky lived through 150 air raids and was a member of the crew that often rescued from the air soldiers who were stranded in the ocean.

Smoky became a hero when she helped build an airstrip so planes could land and take off. The soldiers had to run a wire through a very long pipe—about the length of 12 cars parked end-to-end—and the pipe was only eight inches high and half-filled with soil. None of the soldiers could thread that wire through that pipe. Could Smoky help? Her soldier buddy tied the wire to Smoky and called to her from the far end of the pipe. With grit and determination, Smoky slowly, slowly squeezed through the long, narrow, dirty pipe and came out with the wire at the other end. Thanks to Smoky, the airstrip was built!

After the war, Smoky traveled the world, showing off her tricks, which included walking on a tightrope—blindfolded! She appeared on 42 live TV shows and never once repeated a trick.

American President Richard Nixon had a Yorkie named "Pasha" living with him in the White House.

Origin

Yorkies originated in the rugged Yorkshire region of northern England in the mid-1800s. The breed descends from one particular Yorkie named "Huddersfield Ben." He came from the town of Huddersfield in Yorkshire.

At the height of the Industrial Revolution in England, Yorkies had an important job to do: chase and kill rats (yuck!) at textile mills and coal mines.

Saint Bernard

The Saint Bernard is a giant dog who is famous for his size and for rescuing people trapped in mountain snow.

For hundreds of years, pilgrims walked through the Swiss mountains on their way to Rome, to visit the heart of the Catholic Church and the home of the Pope, called "Vatican Palace."

The snow is very deep in the Swiss mountains and tired pilgrims would often become trapped and covered by snow. Saint Bernards searched for these missing pilgrims. The dogs would go out in pairs, and could tell by their noses where a pilgrim was buried. They would dig in the snow to uncover him. Then one dog would wake up the pilgrim and lay on top of him to keep him warm, while the other dog went back to the nearby monks for help.

During the 200 years that the dogs worked as rescuers in the mountain pass, they saved more than 2,000 people! The last known rescue was in 1897, when a Saint Bernard found a 12-year-old boy nearly frozen in the snow and woke him up.

The most famous Saint Bernard is "Barry." This one dog rescued more than 40 people. He lived from 1800 to 1814. Ever since, the monks in the Swiss mountains always have one dog named "Barry" to honor his memory. The original Barry is on display in the Natural History Museum in the city of Berne, Switzerland, the same way you can see stuffed lions and bears in a museum.

American President Theodore Roosevelt had a good-natured Saint Bernard named "Rollo" living with him in the White House.

Unless a Saint Bernard learns to play with children while he is still a puppy, he can grow up to be too difficult for children to handle. He is sometimes too difficult for a grown-up to handle because he is so huge! But he is a gentle giant who is not aggressive. Instead, he is very eager to please.

Origin

The Saint Bernard dog comes from the Swiss Mountains called the "Alps." He is named after a monk, Saint Bernard, who established a monestary and traveler's lodge in a mountain pass in the Alps over a thousand years ago. The dog, the lodge, and the mountain pass are all named after the monk, Saint Bernard.

In the 1600s, the monks acquired their first dogs to be watchdogs and companions, but they soon discovered the dogs' life-saving abilities.

We often see pictures of the Saint Bernard with a little barrel, or cask, of liquor under his chin. The liquor was meant to keep someone warm who was trapped in the snow, until help arrived. But the monks' diaries don't mention sending their dogs out with these barrels. Historians say that the legend comes from a writer's made-up story and from a famous painting that shows the dogs with casks under their chins. We may never know the truth!

Jack Russell Terrier

The Jack Russell Terrier is a small dog, bold and feisty. He has so much energy, and gets into so much mischief with his playfulness, that he can be hard to handle. He loves to run, dig and bark. Some like to climb trees!

He's not the dog for everyone. You have to be very firm in training him or he'll think he's the boss. And he's not good with young children because he won't put up with any teasing or hitting or play-fighting.

The Jack Russell is good for someone with a sense of humor, who enjoys surprises and the high-jinks that go on with this scamp.

In England, a famous Jack Russell was "Chalky," who appeared on TV with Chef Rick Stein. Chalky was so popular that he had his own line of products for sale, including dolls, kitchen towels, paw prints—and even his own beer!

The most famous Jack Russell in America was the dog character "Eddie" in the TV series, *Frasier*. Because the show ran for so many years, Eddie was played by two different dogs, a father named "Moose" and his son, "Enzo." The dog character, Eddie, received more fan mail than any of the human actors!

Both dogs, father and son, had a rough coat. The Jack Russell can have either a rough or smooth coat, meaning a long or short coat.

There is a famous series of books for kids called *Jack Russell: Dog Detective* that you will enjoy reading.

Origin

The Jack Russell Terrier is named after Reverend John Russell, who was an English parson and fox-hunting fan. "Jack" is a nick-name for "John."

In the mid-1800's, Reverend Russell bought a female terrier named "Trump" from the milkman, and bred his own special line of dogs that were good at chasing a fox into its hole underground and barking so hunters would hear and come get the fox. The Jack Russell has to be very brave and determined to do this.

Dachshund

The Dachshund (say DAHKS-hoond) is a small dog, with short legs and a long body. The writer H. L. Mencken called him "a half-a-dog high and a dog-and-a-half long." The Dachshund's nicknames are "wiener dog," "hotdog dog," and "Doxie."

Here's a riddle for you: Why did the father buy his six children a Dachshund? He wanted a dog they could all pet at once!

The Doxie is lively and friendly. He loves to play fetch, and chase birds and small animals.

With his loud bark, he makes a good watchdog. And this small dog is brave—he'll stand up to much bigger dogs.

He can be hard to train, though. The writer E. B. White joked that "he even disobeys me when I instruct him in something he wants to do." (You may know E. B. White from his children's books, *Stuart Little* and *Charlotte's Web.*)

The Doxie is good with older children who will be careful of his back, which can be easily hurt.

The Doxie comes in two sizes, standard and miniature—that's small and tiny. He also comes in three different kinds of coats: short, long, or wiry.

If you like Doxies, you'll enjoy the books *Hallo-wiener* by Dav Pilkey, *Noodle* by Munro Leaf, and *Pretzel* by H. A. Rey and Margret Rey. (You may know the Reys from the *Curious George* books.)

Older kids and grown-ups will like the book *Wiener Dog Art: A Far Side Collection* by Gary Larson.

A city in Russia has a monument to the Dachshund, and on City Day, July 25th, a parade of Doxies passes by!

A battalion of American soldiers in World War II found a Dachshund and adopted him as their mascot. They named him "Furlough" (say FUR-loh), which means a short vacation from soldier work. The monument built to honor these soldiers even includes a statue of their Doxie mascot!

Origin

The Dachshund comes from Germany. The breed is hundreds of years old, but no one knows for sure how it got started.

The Dachshund was bred to chase badgers into their burrows— "dachs" means "badger" in German. The Doxie has to be very brave to hunt an angry badger!

Dachshunds were favorite pets of European royalty, especially Great Britian's Queen Victoria. She even had a bronze statue made of her Doxie, named "Boy," and displayed it at Windsor Castle! In addition to being hunting dogs, Doxies strolled alongside ladies of fashion in the 1800s.

Because the Dachshund is a symbol of Germany, he was the mascot of the 1972 Summer Olympics held in Munich.

Boxer

The Boxer loves to play with children, and he gets along with other pets at home—even cats! The Boxer is a very popular family dog—even though he snores!

He's medium-sized, full of energy, and loyal and protective.

He is such a great all-around dog that he has worked as a determined hunting dog, a brave police dog, a helpful seeing-eye dog for the blind, a protective guard dog, a daring messenger dog during wartime, and even an entertaining circus dog!

One heroic Boxer was Vittles. "Vittles" is another word for "food." He was named after Operation Vittles, the nickname for the Berlin Airlift that brought food by airplane to people living in West Berlin in Germany in the late 1940s. Why was this Boxer such a hero? Because he flew thousands of hours with the pilots as a crew dog, and even had his own parachute! His lovable nature kept the pilots' spirits up during their long, hard work.

Some famous people who have proudly owned a Boxer include Humphrey Bogart, the star of the movie *Casablanca*, which your grandparents would love to tell you about; Pablo Picasso, the best-known artist of the 20th century; today's race car driver Dale Earnhardt Jr.; and Sylvester Stallone, star of the *Rocky* movies.

Origin

Boxers come from Germany. Boxer-type dogs have been around for hundreds of years, but the breed was standardized by three German gentlemen near the year 1900.

Boxers were excellent hunting dogs who could hold on to a boar, bull or bear until their masters came.

Boxers get their name for the way they stand on their back legs and begin a fight or play-fight by boxing with their paws.

Here's a riddle to ask your friends: What dog goes into a corner every time he hears a bell ring? Answer: a Boxer!

West Highland White Terrier

The nickname for the small West Highland White Terrier is "Westie." He's an adorable, spunky, happy, white fluff of a dog. People say he has a "big personality."

He looks like the kind of dog you could cuddle on your lap, but if you try it, he'll probably scamper off because he's full of energy and very independent. But try playing with him and he'll love it. He won't put up with any ear- or tail-pulling, though, so he does best with an older, more considerate, child.

The Westie likes to dig and bark; his bark makes him a good guard dog.

His small size also makes him a good traveling companion. In fact, it's a good idea to take him with you when you go out because he loves the company of his people and if left alone will be sad, and might get into mischief around the house.

The Westie's coat doesn't shed, so he is good for people with allergies.

Some famous Westies are characters in children's books. Younger children are sure to enjoy the *McDuff* series by Rosemary Wells, and *Good Boy, Fergus!* by David Shannon.

Origin

The Wesite comes from the Highlands of western Scotland.
He was originally bred to hunt foxes and badgers. Legend says
that the breeder, Colonel Malcolm, once had a red terrier who
was mistaken for a fox and accidentally shot. So Colonel Malcolm
insisted that his terrier dogs be bred to be white so they would
stand out and such a tragic mistake would never happen again.
And that's how the all-white Westie got his start, over a hundred
years ago.

Great Dane

The Great Dane is huge and regal, often called the "king of dogs" and a "gentle giant." He is loving and patient, and good with children. But be sure you are watched over by a grown-up since the Great Dane is so large, he can be hard to handle.

One Great Dane named "Gibson" was named the world's tallest dog by the Guinness Book of Records. Gibson was 42 inches high at the shoulders—that's almost as tall as a small pony! He was truly a "gentle giant" because he worked as a therapy dog, visiting sick and sad people in hospitals and nursing homes to cheer them up.

Two other famous Great Danes are the cartoon character Scooby-Doo, and Marmaduke, a character in a comic strip.

The founder of Pennsylvania, William Penn, had a Great Dane as his best friend. When the Pennsylvania Legislature voted in 1965 to name the Great Dane their state dog, they had a "voice vote" and everyone there yipped, growled and barked their approval. The person in charge proclaimed, "The arfs have it!"

American President Franklin Delano Roosevelt—"FDR" for short—had a Great Dane named—guess what?—"President"!

Origin

The Great Dane has a long history. Dogs that look like Great Danes go way, way back to ancient Egypt, about 5,000 years ago. And about 3,000 years ago, the Chinese wrote about dogs like Great Danes. The cruel warrior-king, Attila the Hun, used Great Dane-like dogs to guard his army's camps from the enemy when he invaded Europe about 1600 years ago. The Great Dane that we know today was bred in Germany about 400 years ago to hunt a fierce animal called a wild boar. After the age of sport hunting ended, Great Danes guarded big homes with lots of land, called "estates." Today, the Great Dane's most important job is lovable family dog.

Colors

Great Danes come in six colors: Black; Blue, which is the color of blue-gray steel; Fawn, which is golden yellow with a black face; Brindle, which is golden yellow with black "tiger stripes" on his body; Mantle, which is black and white in this pattern: solid black on his back, sides, and around his head and ears, and white around his neck, chest, muzzle, paws and the tip of his tail; and Harlequin, which is white with irregular black patches. The color Harlequin is named after a clown who has a black and white costume with diamond shapes.

Corgi

The Corgi (say KOR-gee) is short, active and eager to please. If you're a child, he might try to "herd" you by nipping at your heels. But don't worry, you can train him not to do this.

The Corgi has this herding instinct because he was bred to herd cattle. He nipped at the cattle's heels to move them along, and if the cattle kicked back, the Corgi was safe because the hooves went right over the head of the short Corgi!

Legend says that fairies rode Corgis, and that you can still see the fairies' saddle marks on the shoulders of today's Corgis.

There are two kinds of Corgis: the Cardigan, which has a long, bushy tail, and its cousin, the Pembroke, which has no tail. The Pembroke is more popular in the United States.

Corgis are favorite characters in books. Older kids will like *The Courageous Corgi* by Lea Herrick. No matter how old you are, you'll laugh your way through the pictures of Corgi artist Evie Anderson.

The most famous fan of Corgis is Queen Elizabeth II of England—she has about a dozen of them!

Origin

Way back in the year 1107—about 900 years ago—King Henry I of England invited Flemish weavers to set up shop in Pembroke-shire, Wales. The weavers brought their Corgi dogs, where they soon found their natural talent for herding cattle. This is the origin of the Pembroke Corgi.

The Cardigan Corgi goes back even further in the mists of time, to 1200 BC—that's about 3,200 years ago!—when the Celts brought the dog to Cardiganshire in Wales.

The word "Corgi" is Welsh for "dwarf dog."

Bloodhound

The Bloodhound is a big dog with long droopy ears and baggy, saggy folds of skin around his face and neck. Shakespeare wrote that the Bloodhound's ears "sweep away the morning dew."

The Bloodhound is very affectionate and loves children. Be kind to him and he'll be loving and loyal to you.

The Bloodhound is famous for following a scent, even one that is days old. Police use Bloodhounds to track criminals who are hiding, or people who have gone missing. One Bloodhound named "Nick Carter" found over 600 criminals in the early 1900s. In 1954, other Bloodhounds, owned by Norman Wilson, found a boy who had been missing for 332 hours—that's a scent more than 13 days old!

The Bloodhound does *not* get his name from following the scent of blood. Goodness, no! The term "blooded" or "blue-blooded" used to mean aristocratic or noble. And noble the Bloodhound is.

Down through the centures, kings and queens of England and France have loved many Bloodhounds.

You may know "Pluto," a Bloodhound in animated cartoons on television. Another TV Bloodhound is "McGruff the Crime Dog" who "takes a bite out of crime."

Origin

The forerunner of today's Bloodhound can be traced back to the 700s, when a nobleman and keen hunter, Francois Hubert, retired after his wife's death and joined a monestery on the border of Belgium and France. Here, he continued to breed dogs who were known for their ability to track a "cold," or old, scent. Every year, the monestery sent pairs of their hounds to the French king as a tribute—that's how highly valued the dogs were.

After Francois Hubert died, he was named the patron saint of hunters, and to this day, November 3rd is called Saint Hubert's Day, with festivities in France, Belgium and Ireland that include blessing the hounds.

In 1066, William the Conquerer brought St. Hubert hounds with him when he invaded England and claimed the throne. In England, the dogs were called Bloodhounds.

With the turmoil of the French Revolution in the late 1700s, Bloodhounds became nearly extinct there.

The breed was saved by breeders in England, where Edwin Brough firmly established the modern standards and is considered the father of the modern breed. Dog shows began to flourish in the mid-1800s, and even Queen Victoria entered her Bloodhound in a show!

The Bloodhound also found his way to America, as early as Colonial times, and has made his home here as a tracking and companion dog.

Schnauzer

The Schnauzer (say SHNOW-zer—rhymes with OW!-zer) comes in three sizes: large, medium and small, called Giant, Standard and Miniature.

The handsome Schnauzer makes you smile when you see his heavy eyebrows, mustache and beard. He is named for the German word "schnauze," which means "muzzle" or "snout."

The Schnauzer is loyal, active and protective. He loves children and makes a great watchdog.

Schnauzers shed very little, so they're good for people with allergies.

Miniature Schnauzers are very popular as pets in the United States, while Standard Schnauzers are popular in Europe. Even so, Standard Schnauzers are used in the United States to sniff out the location of bombs, to search for and rescue missing people, and even to identify harmful cancer cells that make some people sick.

Martial artist and film star Bruce Lee owned a miniature Schnauzer. Swashbuckling American actor, Errol Flynn, had two Standard Schnauzers who stayed with him on movie sets while he was working.

Origin

The Schnauzer breed started as a German farm dog. He herded sheep and cattle, hunted rats and other vermin, and guarded people and property. He was also good at guarding the carts of traveling tradesmen, filled with work tools, from village to village.

Back in the 1600s, the famous Dutch painter, Rembrandt, painted Schnauzers, and there's even a statue from the 1300s in a German marketplace of a hunter and his Schnauzer.

The Standard size came first. In the late 1800s, the Miniature and Giant sizes were bred from the Standard to be smaller and larger.

Soldiers returning home from the First World War brought Schnauzers with them, which is how this courageous and spirited dog became popular in the United States.

Siberian Husky

On and on and on he runs—pulling a sled—fast! That's the Siberian Husky.

Siberian Huskies have dense fluffy coats and the most beautiful eyes: ice-blue, dark blue, amber, or brown. Sometimes, an individual Siberian Husky will have one eye brown and the other blue, or even both eyes half-brown and half-blue! This has no impact on how well he can see, but looking at the eyes of such a dog is a treat.

Siberian Huskies are friendly and outgoing. Like his close relative, the Wolf, the Siberian Husky howls rather than barks.

Siberian Huskies saved the town of Nome, Alaska in 1925 when a diphtheria epidemic broke out and there was no medicine nearby to treat sick patients. Without medicine, all the sick patients would surely die.

It usually took 25 days for postal mail to be delivered by dog sled from Nenana, Alaska to Nome—a distance of 674 miles. But miraculously, Siberian Huskies carrying their precious cargo of medicine, pulled sleds on the dangerous, freezing trek in Arctic blizzards—in only five days! And that's with temperatures dipping as low as minus 80 degrees Fahrenheit! They delivered the medicine in time and saved Nome, Alaska. The Siberian Huskies were heroes.

The last part of the sled run was led by a dog named "Balto," and a statue of him sits in Central Park in New York City to honor him and all the dogs of the "serum run of 1925."

Origin

Siberian Huskies were originally bred hundreds of years ago by the Chukchi (say CHOOK-chee) people in northeastern Asia on the Siberian peninsula. It is very cold there, with a lot of snow and ice. The Chukchi bred the dogs to pull sleds over long distances, without getting tired. Siberian Huskies have big "snow shoe" feet, with fur between their toes, which keeps them warm and helps them grip the ice.

All Siberian Huskies of today can be traced back to these Chukchi dogs.

Labrador Retriever

The nickname for this big, gentle, friendly dog is "Lab." He is one of the most popular dogs in the United States and is especially loving and loyal to children.

The Lab comes in three different colors: yellow, chocolate or black.

The Lab is eager to please his human companions, and makes an excellent seeing-eye dog for the blind. He also helps firefighters and police find and rescue people who are trapped somewhere such as in a well or under a fallen tree in the woods. The Lab also works with soldiers and police to sniff out explosives. And in yet another side to his personality, he works as a therapy dog, visiting people in hospitals to cheer them up.

Labrador Retrievers are loved around the world. American President Bill Clinton and Russian Prime Minister Vladimir Putin both had Labrador Retrievers.

The star of the book and movie, *Marley and Me*, was a Lab. The story was based on the real life and times, both humorous and touching, of Marley the American Lab. You will love reading *Marley: A Dog Like No Other* by John Grogan, written especially for young people.

Origin

The Labrador Retriever comes from Canada. He was brought to England in the early 1800s, where the breed was firmly established. The American Labrador Retriever is taller, with a lighter build, than the English Lab.

The Lab's paws are webbed for easy swimming, and go back to his original job of retrieving fishing nets.

Jobs with Dogs

When you grow up, you can work with dogs in many different ways. Here are some of them:

Dog Groomer

You get to work with all kinds of dogs, all shapes and sizes. The job involves washing and clipping the coat, and clipping or filing the nails. When the dogs leave your care, they look, smell and feel great, and the owners are happy, too. You can work from home or in a shop.

Dog Trainer

A dog trainer helps both the dog and the dog's owner learn to change their behavior so that problems are solved, and both the dog and owner learn to live together happily. The dog also learns to get along with other dogs and people it comes across during daily walks and in the park, and with people who visit the owner's home. Being a dog trainer is very rewarding work.

Animal Control Officer and Shelter Worker

In many cities, Animal Control Officers are police officers who enforce laws about animals. They teach people about dog care and take stray dogs to the pound. Sometimes they go to court to testify against owners who have broken the law.

An Animal Control Officer may also be a Humane Agent who investigates cruelty to animals, and takes dogs to a shelter to get well and then to be adopted by loving families.

Young people can volunteer at a shelter to feed and groom dogs, play with them and clean their kennels. This is a good way to find out if you would like to work with dogs when you grow up.

Veterinarian

A veterinarian is a doctor for animals. You have to go to school for many years to become a veterinarian. It is very rewarding to heal a sick dog, but a vet's job can also be heartbreaking when a dog is too sick to get better.

Dog Handler

A dog handler takes dogs to dog shows when the owners don't have time to do it themselves. The owners pay the handler to show their dogs. Most dog shows are on weekends. If you like to travel a lot and meet new people (and dogs!), this job is for you. But you have to work very hard to keep a dog in top form and make sure that it performs at its best during the very short time—about two minutes—that the judge is checking the dog in your care. There are even dog shows that teenage handlers can participate in.

Artist and Photographer

Artists draw or paint pictures of dogs that are used in children's books or sold to dog-lovers as gifts. Photographers take pictures of dogs for families and dog show winners.

Index

DOGS: A Kid's Guide to DOG BREEDS
Copyright © Text 2015 Eve Heidi Bine-Stock
Copyright © Illustrations 2015 Jean Batzell Fitzgerald
ISBN 978-0-9831499-3-4
Published by

Eve Heidi Bine-Stock
P.O. Box 3346
Omaha, Nebraska 68103
U.S.A.